D1505934

AMAZING FOOTBALL

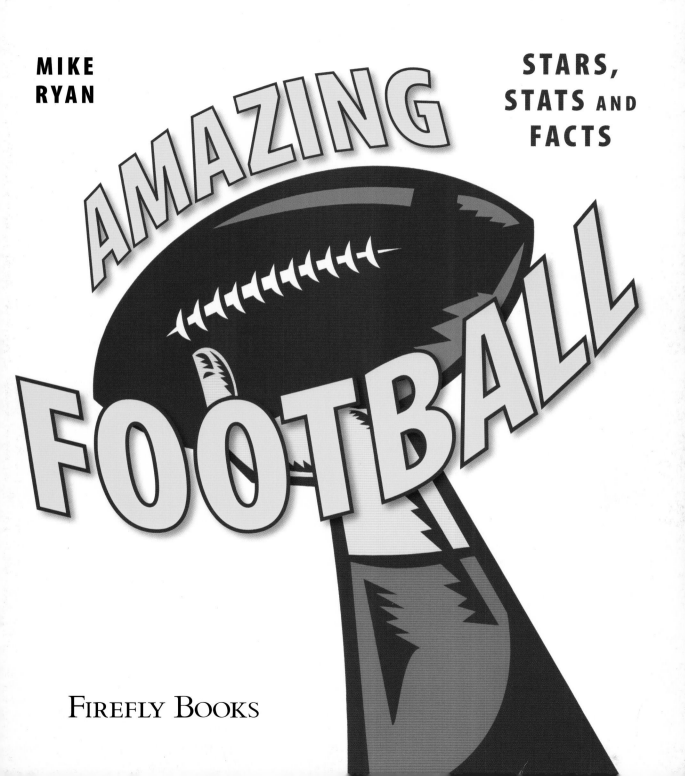

MIKE
RYAN

STARS,
STATS AND
FACTS

AMAZING
FOOTBALL

FIREFLY BOOKS

A FIREFLY BOOK

Published by Firefly Books Ltd. 2016

First printing

Publisher Cataloging-in-Publication Data (U.S.)
Names: Ryan, Mike 1974- , author.
Title: Amazing football : stars, stats and facts / Mike Ryan.
Description: Richmond Hill, Ontario, Canada : Firefly Books, 2016. | Includes index. | Summary: "Profiles of the biggest superstars in today's NFL, as well as a 10-page primer on football" — Provided by publisher.
Identifiers: ISBN 978-1-77085-843-5 (hardcover) | 978-1-77085-777-3 (paperback)
Subjects: LCSH: Football — Biography – Juvenile literature. | National Football League – Biography – Juvenile literature. | Football – Miscellanea – Juvenile literature.
Classification: LCC GV950.7R936 |DDC 796.332 – dc23

Library and Archives Canada Cataloguing in Publication
Ryan, Mike, 1974-, author
Amazing football : stars, stats and facts / Mike Ryan.
Includes index.
ISBN 978-1-77085-843-5 (hardback).—ISBN 978-1-77085-777-3 (paperback)
1. Football players—Biography—Juvenile literature. 2. Football—Juvenile literature. 3. National Football League—Juvenile literature.
I. Title.
GV939.A1R92 2016   j796.332092'2   C2016-902292-7

Published in the United States by
Firefly Books (U.S.) Inc.
P.O. Box 1338, Ellicott Station
Buffalo, New York 14205

Published in Canada by
Firefly Books Ltd.
50 Staples Avenue, Unit 1
Richmond Hill, Ontario L4B 0A7

Cover and interior design: Kimberley Young
Creative Direction: Steve Cameron

Printed in China

The publisher gratefully acknowledges the financial support for our publishing program by the Government of Canada through the Canada Book Fund as administered by the Department of Canadian Heritage.

Table of Contents

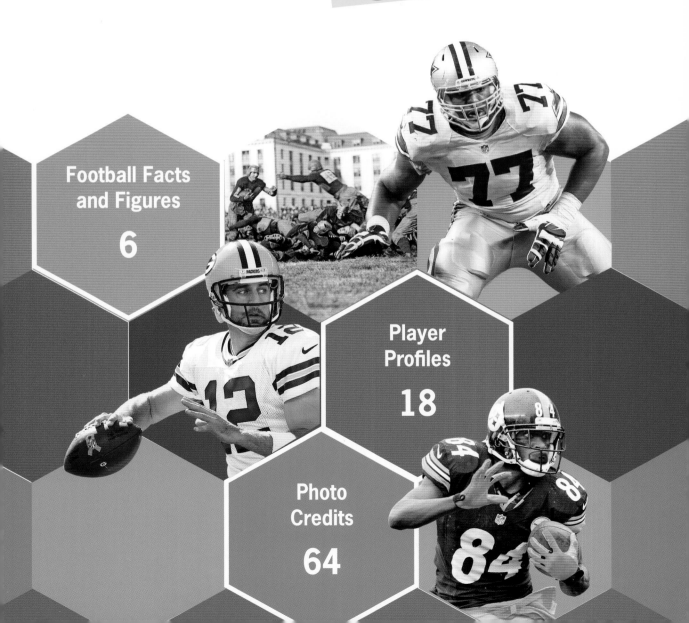

First
and Ten

Football Facts and Figures

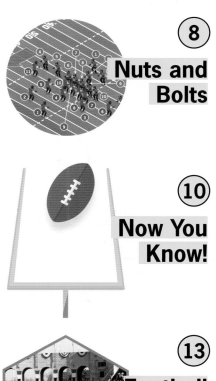

NUTS AND BOLTS

TIME

GAME TIME – 60 minutes split into four 15-minute quarters (15-minute overtime quarters are added as needed)

SEASON – 16 games in an NFL season

PLAYOFFS – four games is the most playoff games a team can play to win the Super Bowl; three games is the least

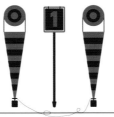

First Down – teams are given four downs (tries) to move the ball 10 yards (or more) in the direction of the opponent's end zone. Every time they move the ball 10 yards, they are rewarded with another four downs to move the ball 10 more yards. If a team fails to move 10 yards in four downs, it is called a "turnover on downs," and the other team gets the ball. The yards needed to achieve a first down are marked by the orange and black yard markers.

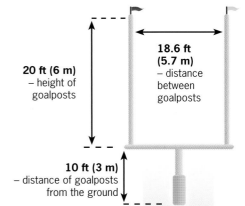

20 ft (6 m) – height of goalposts

18.6 ft (5.7 m) – distance between goalposts

10 ft (3 m) – distance of goalposts from the ground

53.3 yd (48.8 m/160 ft) – width of the field

100 yd (91.4 m/300 ft) – length of the field, goal line to goal line

120 yd (109.7 m/360 ft) – length of the field, including end zones

POINTS

6 **TOUCHDOWN**
Accomplished by running the ball into the end zone or catching the ball in the end zone.

3 **FIELD GOAL**
Accomplished by kicking the ball, which is held in place against the ground by another player, through the goalposts.

2 **TWO-POINT CONVERSION**
(following a touchdown)
Accomplished by running the ball into the end zone or catching the ball in the end zone.

1 **POINT AFTER ATTEMPT**
(following a touchdown)
Accomplished by kicking the ball, which is held in place against the ground by another player, through the goalposts.

2 **SAFETY**
Accomplished by tackling the ball carrier in his own end zone or as a consequence of the offense committing a foul in its own end zone or the ball becoming dead in the offense's end zone (with the exception of an incomplete forward pass).

Maximum number of players each team can have on the field at any one time	**11**
53	Maximum number of players on an NFL roster
Maximum number of players on a game-day roster	**46**

Seven officials call each NFL game:

- referee
- umpire
- head linesman
- line judge
- field judge
- side judge
- back judge

OFFICIALS

DEFENSE

Safety	**1**
Safety	**2**
Outside Linebacker	**3**
Middle Linebacker	**4**
Outside Linebacker	**5**
Cornerback	**6**
End	**7**
Tackle	**8**
Tackle	**9**
End	**10**
Cornerback	**11**

OFFENSE

1	Fullback/Running Back
2	Fullback/Running Back
3	Quarterback
4	Wide Receiver
5	Tight End
6	Tackle
7	Guard
8	Center
9	Guard
10	Tackle
11	Wide Receiver

Now You Know!

Pass the Pigskin?

Footballs are often called "pigskins," but they were, in fact, never made of a pig's skin. In the 19th century balls were often made from animal bladders that were blown up or stuffed, because they were cheap and easy to get. The ball used in the first football game in 1869 was round but lopsided, and the oblong shape stuck and became standard.

Wilson has been the official supplier of balls since 1941, and since 1955, all NFL balls have been made at the Wilson factory in Ada, Ohio. They're made from cowhide from Kansas, Nebraska and Iowa; each cowhide can make about 10 balls. Each ball has four panels and a synthetic bladder to hold air. There is one lace for grip, going through 16 lace holes. Each ball is between 11 and 11¼ inches (28–28.5 cm) long and weighs between 14 and 15 ounces (400–425 grams). It should be inflated to 13 psi. Each team is given 108 game balls per week: 54 for practice and 54 for the game.

What's a Gridiron?

The American football field is often referred to as the "gridiron." In the early days of the game, the lines on the field were more of a grid, like a checkerboard. They looked like the lines on a griddle (the kind used to make waffles), which is the original meaning of the word gridiron. In other countries people sometimes call American football "gridiron football" so as to avoid confusion with football – which North Americans call soccer.

Half a Foot Equals 63 Yards

On November 8, 1970, Tom Dempsey of the New Orleans Saints won the game for his team and set the NFL record with a 63-yard field goal. Setting the record was one thing, but Dempsey did it with a kicking foot that was misshapen at birth and was more of a stump than a foot! The record wasn't broken until 2013, when Matt Prater of the Denver Broncos beat it by one yard.

Gee, That's Interesting!

The "G" on the helmets of the Packers does not stand for Green Bay. In 1961, equipment manager George Braishear came up with the familiar logo, but the letter represented "greatness." It worked: Green Bay won the first two Super Bowls. The University of Georgia liked it so much they used the same logo for their helmets.

11

Paul Hubbard was the quarterback for Gallaudet University (a school for the deaf and hard of hearing in Washington, D.C.). In the 1940s he invented the huddle to make sure that other teams couldn't read their sign language. The huddle is still being used in the NFL.

Football's Oldest, Still Growing Family Tree

In 1899, the Morgan Athletic Club on the south side of Chicago formed a team. It later became the Normals, the Racine Cardinals, the Chicago Cardinals, the St. Louis Cardinals and the Phoenix Cardinals. Today the Morgan Athletic Club is known as the Arizona Cardinals — the oldest continuously running team in pro football.

Footballs Become Airborne

When American football began, players could do three things to advance the ball: run with it, pass it back to a player who would then run with it or kick it forward. The forward pass was first made a legal play in 1906, and the first known forward pass completion in a pro game came on October 25 of that year, when George "Peggy" Parratt of the Massillon Tigers threw a completion to Dan "Bullet" Riley in a win over a combined squad of players from Benwood and Moundsville, West Virginia.

Football Through Time!

1869
Princeton University and Rutgers University face off in a game of "soccer football" using modified rugby rules.

1876
The first rules are created for football.

1892
William "Pudge" Heffelfinger becomes the first player paid to play football: $500 by the Allegheny Athletic Association.

1902
The formation of the first professional football league happens in Pennsylvania.

1906
Players are allowed to pass the ball forward.

1909
Field goals are reduced from four points to three.

1912
Touchdowns are raised from five points to six.

1919
Earl "Curly" Lambeau and George Calhoun form the Green Bay Packers. Lambeau's employer, the Indian Packing Company, provide equipment and a practice field.

1920
The American Professional Football Association is formed after two meetings are held in Canton, Ohio.

1921
Akron Pros player-coach Fritz Pollard becomes the first African-American head coach.

13

1932

1922
The American Professional Football Association becomes the National Football League, and the Chicago Staleys change their name to the Chicago Bears.

1925
Five new franchises join the NFL, including the New York Giants, owned by Tim Mara. The Mara family still owns the Giants.

1929
Ernie Nevers scores six rushing touchdowns and four extra points for a total of 40 points. It is still the NFL record for most points by one player in a single game.

1936
The NFL holds its first draft of college players. Heisman Trophy–winner Jay Berwanger is the first player ever drafted. He never plays in the NFL.

1939
The first Pro Bowl, between NFL-champion New York Giants and a team of All-Stars, is played. The Giants win 13–10.

1939
The first NFL game is televised. NBC broadcasts the Brooklyn Dodgers-Philadelphia Eagles game to about 1,000 TV sets in New York.

1956
The NFL Players' Association is formed.

1959
The rival American Football League is founded with eight franchises.

1963
The Pro Football Hall of Fame opens in Canton, Ohio, with 17 members enshrined.

1965
Americans chose professional football as their favorite sport, overtaking baseball for the first time.

1932
Chicago and Portsmouth play in the first NFL playoff game; because of terrible snow and cold, they play indoors at Chicago Stadium.

1933
The NFL adds inbounds lines, hash marks and goalposts on the goal line. They also legalize the forward pass from anywhere behind the line of scrimmage.

1934
The Chicago-Detroit Thanksgiving Day game becomes the first NFL game broadcast nationally on the radio.

1943
The NFL makes helmets mandatory.

1946
The Cleveland Rams move to Los Angeles.

1948
The NFL gives its referees whistles instead of horns.

1948
Fred Gehrke of the Los Angeles Rams paints horns on the Rams' helmets; the Rams become the first professional team to have helmet emblems.

1967
The NFL and AFL merge, and the NFL's Green Bay Packers beat the AFL's Kansas City Chiefs in Super Bowl I.

1970
Vince Lombardi dies, and the Super Bowl Trophy is renamed the Vince Lombardi Trophy.

Monday Night Football debuts.

1978
The regular season becomes 16 games long, and the NFL adds a second wild-card team to the playoffs.

Dan Marino
Miami

Brent Favre
Green Bay

1983
Super Bowl XVII is the second-highest rated live TV program of all time, giving the NFL all of the top-10 live programs in TV history.

1984
Records set: Dan Marino (Miami Dolphins) passes for 5,084 yards and 48 touchdowns; Eric Dickerson (Los Angeles Rams) rushes for 2,105 yards.

1984
Records set: Art Monk (Washington Redskins) catches 106 passes; Walter Payton (Chicago Bears) breaks Jim Brown's career rushing mark.

1993
The Miami Dolphins' Don Shula becomes the winningest coach in NFL history.

1995
The San Francisco 49ers become the first team to win five Super Bowls, and the NFL becomes the first major sports league to have a website on the Internet.

2000
Minnesota Vikings kicker Gary Anderson passes George Blanda as the NFL's all-time scoring leader, with 2,004 points.

2009
The Pittsburgh Steelers win their record sixth Super Bowl title.

2013
The Denver Broncos' Peyton Manning breaks the single-season records for passing yards (5,477) and touchdowns (55) and becomes the first five-time NFL MVP.

2014
Manning becomes the NFL's all-time leader in career touchdown passes.

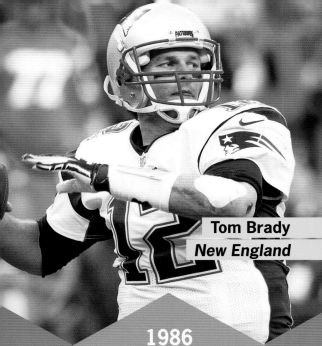

Tom Brady
New England

Peyton Manning
Denver

1986

The telecast of Super Bowl XX becomes the most-viewed television program in history, with an audience of 127 million viewers.

1988

Johnny Grier becomes the first African-American referee in NFL history.

1989

Art Shell is named head coach of the Los Angeles Raiders, becoming the first African-American head coach since Fritz Pollard in 1921.

2002

The Dallas Cowboys' Emmitt Smith becomes the NFL's all-time rushing leader.

2007

Records set: Packers quarterback Brett Favre surpasses Dan Marino in both career passing categories, touchdowns and yards, to become the NFL's all-time leader.

2007

Records set: Patriots quarterback Tom Brady sets the single-season record for TD passes (50); New England becomes the first team ever to finish 16–0 in the regular season.

2015

Manning breaks the NFL record for career passing yards.

2016

On February 7, Super Bowl 50 is played. It's the first time roman numerals aren't used for the Super Bowl.

2016

The Rams move from St. Louis to Los Angeles, 70 years after they moved from Cleveland to Los Angeles.

17

Player Profiles

20 Larry Fitzgerald

28 Greg Olsen

30 Cameron Wake

32 Jimmy Graham

40 Aaron Rodgers

42 Justin Houston

44 Anquan Boldin

52 Jason Witten

54 Richard Sherman

56 Joe Thomas

22 Drew Brees	24 Andrew Luck	26 Antonio Brown
34 Tamba Hali	36 Cam Newton	38 Jamaal Charles
46 J.J. Watt	48 DeMarcus Ware	50 Eli Manning
58 Russell Wilson	60 Thomas Davis	62 Tyron Smith

Larry Fitzgerald plays like a superhero.

Larry Fitzgerald
Arizona Cardinals
Wide Receiver

Larry Fitzgerald plays like a superhero on the football field. The wide receiver is known as "Spidey" for his sticky palms, which help him make spectacular catches, but he could also be called "Wolverine" for his ability to play through pain and heal quickly from injuries.

Fitzgerald's extraordinary powers were first revealed to the football world when he was in college. Playing for the Pittsburgh Panthers in 2003, he was named the best wide receiver in NCAA football — and he did it with a torn ligament in his right hand.

The Arizona Cardinals liked the tough, sure-handed wide-out, and they drafted him third overall in 2004. By the end of the 2005 season, Spidey was the youngest receiver in NFL history to reach 100 receptions. His total of 103 set a Cardinals team record.

In 2008 Fitzgerald became just the fourth receiver in NFL history to have at least 1,400 receiving yards in three or more seasons. In that year's playoffs he took his game to the next level, setting all-time NFL playoff records for catches (30), yards (546), touchdowns (seven) and touchdown catches in consecutive games (four). But it was in the last 11 minutes of Super Bowl XLIII, against the Pittsburgh Steelers, that he was truly super. Fitzgerald caught six passes for 115 yards and two touchdowns. Only one receiver had more yards in an *entire* game against Pittsburgh that whole season!

Fitzgerald's second touchdown gave the Cardinals a 23–20 lead with 2:37 left in the game, but Arizona's luck ran out as Steelers quarterback Ben Roethlisberger marched his team down the field and scored with 35 seconds left to win the Super Bowl.

Fitzgerald revealed that, unbelievably, he set his records with a broken left thumb and torn cartilage in his left hand.

Fitzgerald shares more than his sticky palms and nickname with the blue and red webslinger: like Spider-Man, he lost a loved one when he was younger. His mom died when he was in college, and he hasn't cut his hair since. He braids it as a tribute to her.

Humble and kind like his mother, Fitzgerald — the youngest player to reach 11,000 yards, 80 touchdowns and 900 receptions in NFL history — gets excited when kids wear his Cardinals jersey: "It's an honor and a privilege. I see all the No. 11s out there and I want to make sure I set a good example … it's not all about football. You have to be a good citizen and give back to people less fortunate. Those are things my parents taught me."

SUPER DUDE

In an NFL player vote, Fitzgerald was named as one of the nicest guys in the league. His First Down Fund fixes fields and donates sports equipment in Minnesota and gives laptops to kids in Minneapolis and Phoenix. He also runs the Carol Fitzgerald Memorial Fund, in honor of his mother, to support breast cancer awareness.

Drew Brees
New Orleans Saints Quarterback

At the end of the 2005 NFL season, a lot of people thought Drew Brees' career as a starting quarterback might be done. Playing for the San Diego Chargers, Brees tore up his throwing shoulder in the last game of the season. Surgery fixed his arm, but the Chargers had quarterback-of-the-future Philip Rivers on the roster, so they released Brees from the team.

Earlier that year, Hurricane Katrina had devastated the city of New Orleans. Almost 2,000 people had died, and the Superdome — the New Orleans Saints' stadium — had become a shelter for people who'd lost their homes. Because of that, the Saints played their home games away from home. They ended the 2005 season with a 3–13 record, but that offseason they signed Brees.

"[My wife and I] were brought here for a reason," Brees said.

Brees and his wife, Brittany, rebuilt an old home in downtown New Orleans and started to help others rebuild their lives. They set up the Brees Dream Foundation to help fight cancer; they built playgrounds and repaired football fields.

And Brees' repaired shoulder turned the Saints around on the field — the team finished with a 10–6 record in 2006. By the conclusion of the 2009 season, the Saints were Super Bowl champions. Super Bowl XLIV, a 31–17 win over the Indianapolis Colts, was New Orleans' first championship ever. Brees won the MVP award!

The next season, with a game to spare, Brees beat Dan Marino's 27-year-old single-season record for passing yards. He finished the season with 5,476 yards and set records for completions in a season (468) and completion percentage (71.2 percent).

In 2014 Brees completed 456 passes for 4,952 yards, 33 touchdowns and a 97.0 passer rating. He was first in the NFL in completions and attempts, and he tied for first in passing yards and second in completion percentage. It was his ninth consecutive season of at least 4,000 yards passing — a record — and he made it to his ninth Pro Bowl.

Since arriving in New Orleans in 2006, Brees has only missed two games and leads the NFL in passing yards, completions and touchdowns. He's the most accurate passer in NFL history, and he's the only one with seven straight years throwing at least 30 touchdown passes. He also had a streak of 54 straight games with a touchdown pass, which smashed a record that had stood since 1960.

Brees has been named NFL Man of the Year and *Sports Illustrated* Sportsman of the Year. He holds all of New Orleans' quarterback records, and it is safe to say he holds a special place in the city's heart and history.

SAY WHAT? | Brees is the only player in NFL history to throw for at least 5,000 yards in a season more than once. He's done it four times!

Drew Brees
always hits
his target.

Andrew Luck
Indianapolis Colts
Quarterback

Being drafted first overall comes with a lot of pressure. NFL clubs expect a number-one draft pick to step on the field as a rookie and make their team better right away. Living up to those expectations is very difficult. For Andrew Luck of the Indianapolis Colts, that was only half of it. He also had to make the fans in Indianapolis forget that Peyton Manning, one of the greatest quarterbacks of all time, had left town.

Luck isn't like other players though. His father, Oliver, is a former NFL quarterback, and while there are many players (including Manning) whose dads played pro, not many of them also managed football teams in Europe.

Young Andrew lived in England and Germany before his family moved back to the United States, and he grew up with a view of the bigger world. He learned international customs, went to different schools and was surrounded by culture and history and different languages.

Another thing that sets Luck apart is that school was just as important as football to him. In high school he was a star quarterback as well as co-valedictorian. When it came time to go to college, he chose Stanford University because it's one of the top colleges and would give him an excellent education.

The season before Luck enrolled, Stanford's football team had finished 1–11. As an architectural design major, Luck won 31 of the 38 games he played, and he recorded the most wins by a quarterback in the school's history. Even though he was ready for the NFL after his junior year, he returned to complete his degree and play his senior season in 2011.

That same year the NFL's Colts were 2–14 — the worst record in the league. Manning, their All-Pro quarterback, had missed the entire season after having neck surgery, and the Colts released him from the team before the 2012 season.

In the 2012 draft, Indianapolis picked Luck first overall to replace Manning. He led them to an 11–5 record and set an NFL rookie record with 4,374 yards passing. Luck now holds the league record for the most yards in a quarterback's first three seasons (12,957) and has the most passing yards for any quarterback in their first five playoff games (1,703). In 2014 he broke Manning's single-season franchise yardage record by throwing for 4,761 yards.

Luck and Manning are respected league-wide for their sportsmanship. Manning, who retired after winning the Super Bowl in 2016, holds most of the all-time regular season quarterback records, but Luck might have him beat in niceness. He congratulates opponents for a good play after he's been sacked or hit really hard. It is a gesture so rare that defenders don't know how to react.

In a world of trash talk and aggression, Luck's kind attitude might be the most genius football move of all.

FOOTIE FANATIC | Growing up in England and Germany made Luck a big fan of soccer, which is called football in Europe. He goes to Europe to watch soccer games and followed the American team in Brazil at the 2014 World Cup.

Antonio Brown
Pittsburgh Steelers
Wide Receiver

84

Antonio Brown grew up in a rough part of Miami, sometimes without a place to sleep. His dad — "Touchdown" Eddie Brown — was named the best player in Arena Football League history, but he wasn't around to help raise his son.

Brown's dream was to play in the NFL, but without a mom and dad to support him, his school grades suffered. "I wasn't a kid who got in trouble [or] did anything wrong," Brown says, "I just was a guy who didn't really have the right guidance in place and the right support [to help me do] the things that I wanted to do."

In high school Brown was one of the best sprinters in Florida and an All-State quarterback, even though he was so skinny he was called "Boney Tony." His small size and poor grades meant he didn't receive any scholarship offers to play football in college, but Boney Tony wasn't giving up.

Brown worked on his school skills and eventually landed a tryout with Central Michigan University as a wide receiver. He made it, and a few weeks later he was offered a scholarship. Brown went on to become the only player in Central Michigan history to have two 1,000-yard receiving seasons and two 100-reception seasons.

Brown was still scrawny though, so he didn't get picked until the sixth round of the 2010 NFL draft. The Pittsburgh Steelers took him 195th overall. He sat on the bench for seven games in his rookie year.

"You've got to be patient," says Brown. "Patience builds perseverance and it builds humility and it teaches you a lot."

His patience was rewarded in the playoffs. Despite not starting any games, Brown made two unbelievable catches that helped the Steelers reach Super Bowl XLV. One catch he held against his helmet to help beat the Baltimore Ravens, and the other he caught on his knees to seal a victory over the New York Jets.

The Steelers lost to the Green Bay Packers in the Super Bowl, but the next year Brown became the first player in NFL history with at least 1,000 receiving yards and 1,000 return yards in the same season!

In 2013 Brown set a team record with 1,499 receiving yards and had the second-most receptions (110) in team history. In 2014 he blew those numbers away and led the NFL with 1,698 yards and 129 receptions.

Brown says the secret to his success is hard work and making the right decisions: "You have to be professional on and off the field."

If you are, you can go from being a skinny kid with nowhere to sleep to one of the most reliable receivers in the NFL — and a YouTube star.

FIVE-50 CLUB

In 2013 Brown became the first player in NFL history to have at least five receptions and 50 receiving yards in all 16 games of the regular season. He did it again in 2014.

Antonio Brown can't be contained.

Greg Olsen
Carolina Panthers
Tight End

88

NFL general managers don't usually admit they made a bad trade. Jerry Angelo was the Chicago Bears GM who drafted Greg Olsen in the first round in 2007. Four years later Angelo traded him to the Carolina Panthers for a third round pick.

"That's on me," confessed Angelo. "You don't let your best player — one of your better players — out the door. Everything he's doing hasn't surprised me. He's an excellent player."

Olsen's high school coach wouldn't have traded him. It was his dad, Chris, and together, father and son led Wayne Hills High School in New Jersey to the 2002 state title. It was Greg's senior year, and he was a First Team All-American.

Despite his high school success, Olsen wasn't expected to get much playing time when he joined the powerhouse University of Miami in 2004, but he slowly worked his way up, impressing the Miami coaches with the football smarts that he and his father had worked on in high school. In his second year at Miami he appeared in 12 games, and in his third he led the Hurricanes with 40 catches. That year, the Bears drafted him in the first round.

The 2011 trade to Carolina took Olsen by surprise. He called it "bittersweet" but said he was happy to "go play somewhere where I feel like I have a better opportunity."

He took that opportunity and ran with it. Olsen set Carolina franchise records for the most single-season catches (69) and receiving yards (843) by a tight end. He upped his receptions and led the Panthers with 73 in 2013 and 84 in 2014. In 2014 Olsen also broke the 1,000-yard reception mark and made his first Pro Bowl team!

And so, before the 2015 season, Olsen decided that he was going to be a Panther for life, signing a contract with Carolina that will see him through to retirement.

Aside from his success on the field, Olsen's decision was a personal one. When his son Trent Jerry (TJ) was born with a heart defect and needed surgery to live, Carolina team owner Jerry Richardson (whom TJ is partly named after) flew the family to Boston on his private jet to see a doctor and later sat with them during TJ's surgery. Afterward, Olsen and his wife, Kim, set up The Heartest Yard foundation in Charlotte to help kids like TJ.

"Playing football in the NFL is stressful enough," says TV analyst Cris Collinsworth, a former NFL receiver, "But to be able to balance his other duties as a husband and father so well really tells you all you need to know about Greg Olsen.

"I think we are all going to be remembered and judged on what we do away from football, and Greg Olsen is getting it right."

CLUTCH CATCHES | Olsen is the only tight end in the NFL with five or more receiving touchdowns every year since 2008.

Greg Olsen shoulders the load.

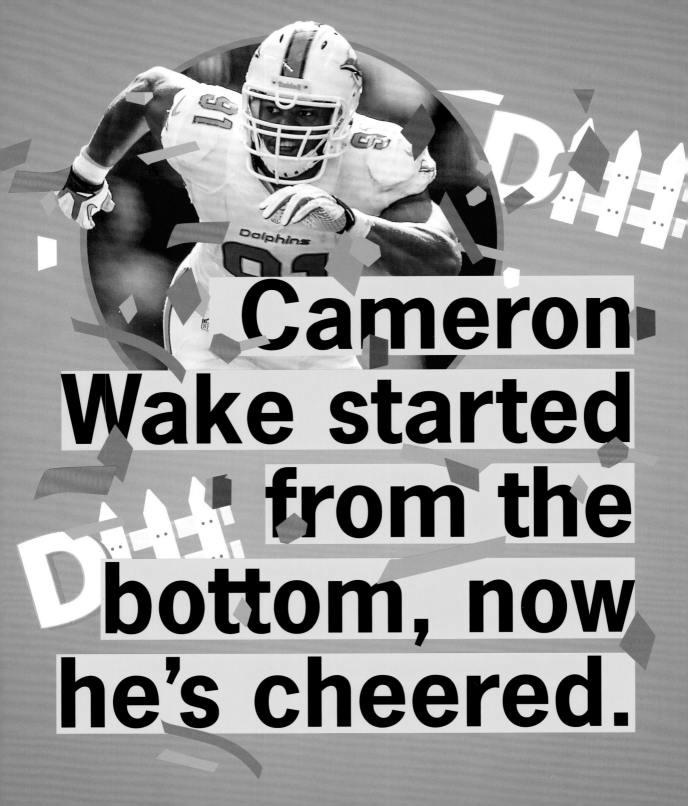

Cameron Wake started from the bottom, now he's cheered.

Cameron Wake
Miami Dolphins
Defensive End

Once upon a time, a man named Derek worked in a little cubicle, in a dull one-story building, in a quiet suburb of Baltimore. At 6-foot-3 and 262 pounds, Derek didn't look like an office worker, and he didn't want to be one either.

He sat at a desk for eight hours a day, but he also spent four more hours in the gym. He dreamt of being a football player, so he decided to quit his day job and work full time at the gym to get in shape. The gym was also where he started to go by his middle name, Cameron. The switch represented a fresh start.

Skip forward a few years, and Cameron Wake's dream has come true. He's sack master for the Miami Dolphins.

As unlikely as Wake's success story is, it's even more impressive because he didn't play football until his third year of high school. If he hadn't gotten cut from the basketball squad he may never have even tried football. In Wake's two years of high school football, he excelled and earned a scholarship to Penn State University.

Wake was good enough in college to start all four years there, but NFL scouts didn't think he was good enough to be drafted. They just didn't think he was big enough to be on the defensive line in the pros.

After a failed free-agent tryout with the New York Giants, Wake got his office job. He got his second shot at pro football while he was working at the gym. It was north of the border in the Canadian Football League, with the BC Lions, where Wake was named both Rookie of the Year and Most Outstanding Defensive Player in

2007. He is still the only player in CFL history to win both in the same season, and he won Most Outstanding Player again in 2008.

Wake had 39 sacks during his two seasons in Canada, and NFL teams took notice. Nine teams were fighting for his services for the 2009 season, and the Miami Dolphins won the bidding war, signing him to a four-year contract.

Wake made a tackle on the opening kickoff of the first game of his NFL career, and in 2010 he finished third in the league with 14.0 sacks.

In 2012 Wake moved to defensive end. He was fourth in the league with 15.0 sacks, and he made his first appearance on the All-Pro first team. He's now been on three All-Pro teams and played in four Pro Bowls, but he still wears the dirty, old shower sandals that he was given on his first day in the CFL.

"The sandals are a simple reminder never to get complacent, always be humble," says Derek Cameron Wake. "It's not where you start, it's where you finish. Whatever's made me into me, I'm not too upset about it."

HIT THE SACK

Wake had 63.0 sacks from 2009 through 2014. It was the most sacks by any Dolphin in his first six seasons and the fourth most sacks by any NFL player in those same six seasons.

Jimmy Graham
Seattle Seahawks
Tight End

When Jimmy Graham was 11 years old, his mother decided she couldn't raise him alone and left him at an orphanage. He was always going hungry in the children's home, so when he found a local church that gave out free food, he became a regular.

Becky Vinson taught bible classes at the church and started to look after Graham. She taught him the value of hard work and the importance of school. If he didn't get good grades he didn't get to play basketball — his favorite sport.

"People looked at Jimmy as a problem kid," says Vinson, "but I knew there was something more to him."

Graham was a basketball star and earned a scholarship to play at the University of Miami. His college coach called him the best defender he ever had. He was offered tryouts with nine NBA teams and a contract in Spain. He even got a call from the NFL's New England Patriots, even though he hadn't played football since the ninth grade.

The Patriots offered Graham $5,000 to sign immediately, but Miami's football coaches convinced him to try a season of college football with them. His first three catches were all touchdowns. The New Orleans Saints liked his raw talent and drafted him in the third round — 95th overall — in 2010.

After scoring five touchdowns in his rookie year, Graham was one of two players to break the single-season tight-end yardage record in 2011. (The Patriots' Rob Gronkowski had 17 yards more than Graham and set the new record.)

Since 2011, Graham has had more touchdowns, receptions and receiving yards than any other tight end. He was also first on the Saints in receptions for four straight seasons and holds all of the Saints' tight-end receiving records.

In 2014 the Seattle Seahawks had been one pass away from a second Super Bowl title in a row. After the Super Bowl loss, they decided they needed a player like Graham, so they traded for him.

Leaving friends and the only NFL team he had ever played for upset Graham. A quiet and thoughtful guy off the field, he remembers moments like the trade when he gets on the field: "Once I get out there, I'm a different person. I guess it's the little kid inside me who had to fight for everything he's got. And so every Sunday, I fight — it's hard to describe just how much emotion I play with on game day."

JET SETTER

Graham has a pilot's license. In addition to playing professional football, he works as a stunt pilot and flies patients to hospitals.

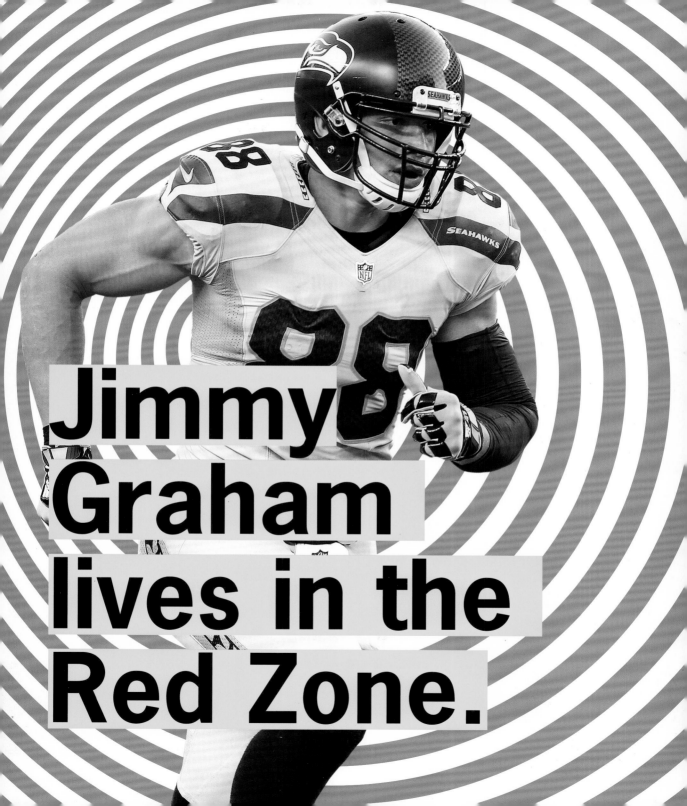

Jimmy Graham lives in the Red Zone.

Tamba Hali defies the odds.

Tamba Hali
Kansas City Chiefs Linebacker

Everyone takes a different path to the NFL, but it doesn't usually start in the African jungle.

Tamba Hali was born in Liberia. When he was six a war broke out in the African country, and his family had to hide among the trees. In 1994 he escaped with his sister and two half-brothers to a neighboring country called the Ivory Coast. Eventually they managed to get halfway across the world to New Jersey to live with their father. Their mother had never officially married their dad, so she wasn't able to go to the United States with the family.

Hali had never been to school before, and he had a hard time reading and writing. He was teased about his accent too, but once he found the football field he felt like he belonged: "Just being out there, having fun with my teammates … But I didn't even know about college scholarships. I was just playing to play."

Hali was offered a scholarship to Penn State University, also known as "Linebacker University" for the linemen the program graduates into the NFL. At Penn State he was an All-American and the Big Ten Defensive Lineman of the Year in 2005. If that didn't impress NFL teams, his speech at the 2006 draft combine did.

"I was just overwhelmed, not only with his story, but the way he told it," said New York Giants general manager Ernie Accorsi. "He's such a thoughtful, intellectual, moving person."

The Kansas City Chiefs drafted Hali 20th overall in 2006, the same year he became an American citizen. It was also the year Hali

saw his mother for the first time since he was 10 years old — a span of 13 years!

"I'm playing for her," Hali said before she was able to come to the United States. "Every time I get to the ball, every time I make my name more known, I feel like I'm closer to her."

As a rookie playing defensive end, Hali led the Chiefs with eight sacks. A move to outside linebacker in 2010 allowed him to have a breakout year, recording 14.5 sacks to lead the AFC.

From 2011 through 2014 Hali missed only two games. He played 91 at outside linebacker and 50 at defensive end. He made the Pro Bowl every year from 2011 to 2014 and has been an All-Pro twice.

"I believe in working," says Hali. "Me impressing myself is not really important. It's about working. Since I've been here, you really just don't say much, and you work, so success is going to come."

DROP THE BEAT | Hali has a recording studio in his basement, where he writes and records his own music.

Cam Newton
Carolina Panthers
Quarterback

Cam Newton loves to play football, and he's always been really good at it. After graduating from Westlake High School in Atlanta, Georgia, he had more than 40 scholarship offers.

Most schools wanted Newton to be a tight end, but Blinn College in Brenham, Texas, knew he could do more. And with some encouragement and faith in Newton's skill, they placed him at quarterback, where he led them to the national junior college championship. After that, Division I Auburn University wanted him to lead their squad.

Newton had one of the best Division I seasons ever. He broke a bunch of school records, won the Heisman Trophy and brought Auburn its first national title since 1957.

The Carolina Panthers snapped him up with the number-one pick in 2011, and in his first NFL game he threw for 422 yards. That broke Peyton Manning's record for most yards in a player's first game.

And he could run, too. Newton set the record for rushing touchdowns by a quarterback with 14 that season. He was also the first quarterback in history with over 4,000 yards passing and 500 yards rushing in a season.

As a club, the Panthers came together around Newton. In 2013 they were 12–4 and won the NFC South title, and in 2014 they were the first team in the NFC South to repeat.

Before the 2015 season, a reporter asked Newton if he was "the NFL's greatest talent as well as the NFL's greatest unknown." After that season those questions were easy to answer: definitely yes and not any more.

The Panthers were 15–1 in the 2015 regular season, and they had fun winning (even if they did lose in the Super Bowl). With Newton as their leader, the team celebrated touchdowns with group poses while Newton did his best Superman impressions. Newton had reason to celebrate: Carolina was the NFL's top-rated offense, and he had 35 touchdown passes and 10 rushing touchdowns. With all that scoring there was also plenty of "Dabbin" — the dance move was one of his favorite celebrations. Newton didn't invent the Dab, but Migos, the rap group who created the dance move, have called him the "Dab Daddy."

Some people thought Newton was disrespecting the game or opponents with the move, which has the dancer's head tuck into the crook of his elbow, but he was just having fun and enjoying a historic season. MVP voters didn't hold it against him either — he got 48 out of 50 votes to win the 2015 award.

Now everybody knows his name, and everybody's Dabbin.

OVER LAND AND THROUGH THE AIR

Newton is the first player in NFL history with at least 3,000 passing yards and 500 rushing yards in four straight seasons, and he's done it five times and counting!

Cam Newton is a touchdown machine.

Jamaal Charles was born to run.

Jamaal Charles
Kansas City Chiefs
Running Back

P ort Arthur is a tough Texas town, with gangs and drugs. Growing up there, Jamaal Charles took special education classes because of a learning disability. The odds of Charles succeeding were stacked against him, but the strong women in his life believed in him. It also helped that he could run like the wind.

Together, his mother, grandmother and aunt kept Jamaal in school and in sports. He won a bronze medal in the 400-meter hurdles at the 2003 World Youth Championships, and he was almost unstoppable on the football field for Memorial High School.

But coaches still underestimated the quiet young man. Because of his troubles in school they doubted he could handle college classes, but his dedication to his studies paid off when he became a Big 12 All-Academic player for the University of Texas. As a freshman, he also helped the Longhorns win the 2005 national title.

Charles was expected to be a late first-round pick in the 2008 NFL draft, but he wasn't taken until the third round. As he waited for his name to be called he cried in private. The Kansas City Chiefs took Charles 73rd overall, and he won the starting running back job partway through his second year. He made sure no one would take it from him. He ran for over 100 yards in each of the final four games of the 2009 season, and in the last game he set a single-game team record with 259 yards rushing.

The following season Charles was a First Team All-Pro and was named to the Pro

Bowl after rushing for 1,467 yards.

In 2011 he tore the ACL in his left knee, but he came back even stronger and led the NFL in touchdowns, with 19, in 2013.

In 2014 he became the third player in history to have at least five seasons of 1,000 yards rushing and a 5.0-yard average per carry. No other active player has done it more than twice!

Charles tore the ACL in his right knee in 2015, but as he's shown in the past, nothing can keep him down for long, and he will work his hardest. He'll do it for his team and because it was the example set for him when he was young.

Charles still goes back to Port Arthur every offseason to run a football camp, and he gives scholarships to students with learning disabilities.

"[My grandma] inspired a lot of people with the way she carried herself. The only thing I can go by is how I inspire people by the way I play. I wanted to inspire little kids to look at me and do [things] the right way."

CRAZY GOOD | In a 2013 game, Charles became the first player in NFL history to have four receiving touchdowns and one rushing touchdown in the same game.

Aaron Rodgers is cool under pressure.

Aaron Rodgers
Green Bay Packers
Quarterback

Aaron Rodgers was a skinny kid with huge feet (size 14!) and a strong arm. As the senior quarterback at Pleasant Valley High School in Chico, California, he set a school record for passing yards. He had a great season, but only one college coach was interested in him, and that coach just had to cross the street to invite him to camp.

Neighbor Craig Rigsbee coached at tiny Butte College a few miles away, in Oroville, California. In Rodgers' one season there, he led the Roadrunners to a 10–1 record. Division I University of California, Berkeley, liked what they saw and invited Rodgers to play on the big stage. He became the highest rated passer in the school's history.

It's a good thing Rodgers has big feet, because he had big cleats to fill in Green Bay after the Packers picked him 24th overall in the 2005 draft. At the time, Green Bay quarterback Brett Favre had played every game for 16 seasons, won three NFL MVP awards and set NFL career records for completions, yards and touchdowns.

But Rodgers was used to proving himself, and in 2008 the Packers handed him the job after a messy split with Favre. Two years later, Rodgers led Green Bay to a 31–25 win over the Pittsburgh Steelers in Super Bowl XLV. He was named the game's MVP.

The Packers didn't repeat as champions in 2011, but Rodgers took his game to another level. The same year Tom Brady and Drew Brees both broke Dan Marino's 27-year-old passing record, Rodgers won the regular-season MVP award. He did it by setting the single-season quarterback rating record of 122.5, with 45 touchdowns and only six interceptions, as the Packers finished 15–1.

Wisconsin's state assembly celebrated by naming December 12, 2012, Aaron Rodgers Day. That year he also ranked third in an American popularity poll, behind Jesus and Abraham Lincoln but ahead of George Washington, Martin Luther King Jr. and Santa Claus.

However, success leads to sky-high expectations. A slow start in 2014 had Packers fans pushing the panic button. Rodgers went on his weekly radio show and told fans to "R-E-L-A-X. Relax. We're going to be okay." Sure enough, the Packers won 11 of their next 13 games and the NFC North title, and Rodgers was named MVP for the second time.

Rodgers was also one of the three finalists for the Walter Payton Man of the Year Award and won the Bart Starr Award in 2014, which is given to the player who best exhibits outstanding character and leadership on the field and in the community.

The scrawny kid who went to the little school has ended up the biggest star in the most popular sport in America.

BRAWN & BRAINS!

In 2015, Rodgers beat Kevin O'Leary from *Shark Tank* and astronaut Mark Kelly on *Celebrity Jeopardy!* to win $50,000 for the Midwest Athletes Against Childhood Cancer (MACC) Fund.

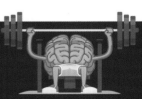

Justin Houston
Kansas City Chiefs
Linebacker

50

Justin Houston grew up in the middle of a family of 10, and they all lived in a small house in Statesboro, Georgia. One evening when Houston was in the ninth grade, he was baby-sitting two of his younger brothers when the house caught on fire. He rushed out in a panic before realizing his siblings were still inside. Even though he couldn't see and could barely breathe, he ran back into the burning house and saved his brothers.

Now more than a decade later, Houston's an All-Pro linebacker for the Kansas City Chiefs, and for a long time his teammates had no idea he was a hero. Houston doesn't like to brag, or really talk about himself at all. He's one of the best players in the NFL, but his quiet nature means he'd never tell anyone that.

After helping Statesboro High School win the state title in 2005, Houston went to the University of Georgia so he could stay close to his family. In his junior year in 2010 he was named team MVP and a First Team All-American.

Football analysts figured Houston's talent could make him a first-round pick in the 2011 NFL draft, but that same talent allowed him to slack off. NFL teams were worried that he didn't have a strong work ethic, and he wasn't chosen until the third round.

In the NFL a player can't survive on talent alone, and Houston worked hard to prove his critics wrong. He played all 16 games and won the Mack Lee Hill Award, given to the Chiefs' best rookie or first-year player.

In 2014, Houston's fourth year, he had four sacks in the season finale to give him 22.0 for the year. It was the most in the NFL that season, and his mark set a new Chiefs record. It was also only half a sack short of Michael Strahan's all-time NFL record for sacks in a season.

But Houston contributes more than just sacks. Kansas City relies on him to shut the door on running backs and to drop back to defend speedy receivers too.

With character and commitment paving his way to stardom, Houston has been able to give back to his family. Now, every Christmas, Houston buys everyone a new pair of shoes. New shoes were a luxury when Houston was a boy, as there were a lot of feet in the family and a lot of footwear to buy.

Houston earned a big contract in 2015, but he didn't get himself anything fancy, like most young superstars do. Instead, he bought his mom and grandmother land so he could build them each a new house.

In a way, he's replacing the house that burned down. And now they all have a place to put their new shoes.

SACK HAPPY | Only seven players in NFL history have had more sacks in their first four seasons than Houston's 48.5. He's also one of just 10 players ever with 20 or more sacks in a season.

Justin Houston's play does the talking.

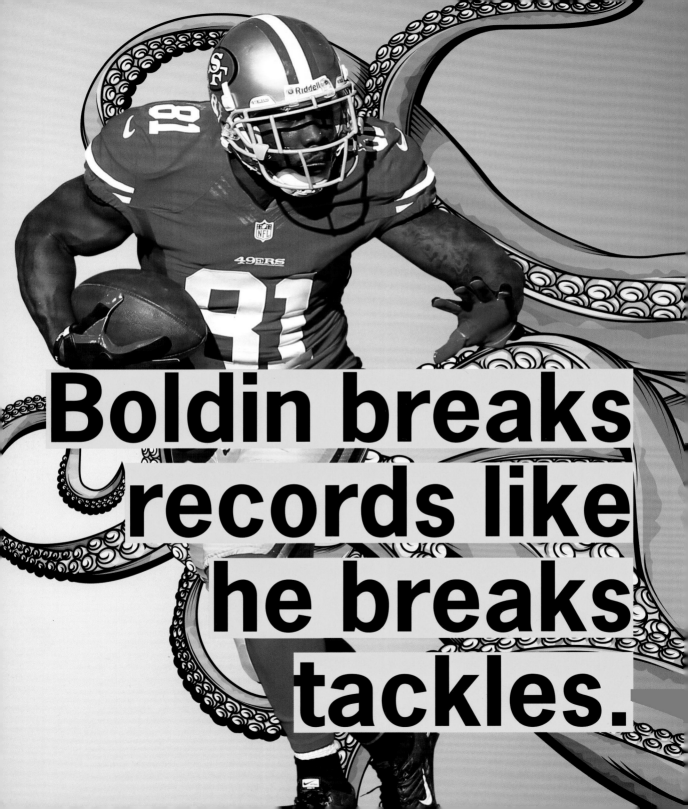

Boldin breaks records like he breaks tackles.

Anquan Boldin
San Fransico 49ers
Wide Receiver

Growing up in Pahokee, Florida, Anquan Boldin's family had a lot of love but very little money. "The good thing about growing up in Pahokee is that we didn't know we were poor because everyone was," he jokes.

His parents were tough but fair, and they expected Anquan and his three brothers and sisters to work hard at everything they did, especially schoolwork. They wanted their kids to get out of Pahokee but never forget where they came from. As Boldin says, "Even if I didn't make it into the NFL, giving back is something that is close to my heart."

He did make it, however, and his football stardom began after he won Florida Player of the Year and Mr. Football in his senior season at Pahokee High School. He even made the state's high school All-Century Team at the "utility" position. When he arrived at Florida State University, he was a star receiver and played quarterback when needed.

Boldin was drafted in the second round by the Arizona Cardinals in 2003, and in his very first game he set an NFL rookie record with 217 receiving yards. By the end of the season he had the league record for receptions by a first-year player — with 101 — and was named the Offensive Rookie of the Year!

Boldin was the Cardinals' all-time leader in receptions when he was traded to the Baltimore Ravens in 2010. He had 104 yards and a touch-down catch in the Ravens' Super Bowl XLVII win following the 2012 season, and he now holds the Ravens' franchise records for

playoff receptions, receiving yards and touchdowns.

Boldin was then traded to the San Francisco 49ers — the team the Ravens had just beaten in the Super Bowl — in the offseason. He found out when he was in the African country of Senegal doing charity work with Oxfam America. Later that same year, he got to tell the U.S. Congress about the work he did in Senegal.

In 2014 Boldin became the second player in history to have 600 or more receiving yards in each of his first 12 seasons. Former 49er and Hall of Famer Jerry Rice was the first. But his reception total probably wasn't what Boldin was most proud of in 2014.

That year, he donated $1 million toward college scholarships, granted through his Q81 Foundation, which helps underprivileged kids get an education. The NFL Players' Association then gave him $100,000 for winning the 2014 Byron "Whizzer" White Award — given to the player who best displays service to his team, community and country.

"Where I come from, there's not much opportunity," explains Boldin. "I try to create opportunity for those that don't have it."

FAST TRACK TO GREATNESS

Boldin reached 400, 500 and 600 receptions faster than any player in NFL history. He's also the first player in NFL history with 50 or more receptions in each of his first 12 seasons.

J.J. Watt
Houston Texans Defensive End

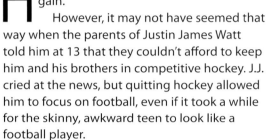

99

Hockey's loss was football's gain.

However, it may not have seemed that way when the parents of Justin James Watt told him at 13 that they couldn't afford to keep him and his brothers in competitive hockey. J.J. cried at the news, but quitting hockey allowed him to focus on football, even if it took a while for the skinny, awkward teen to look like a football player.

At high school in Pewaukee, Wisconsin, Watt was a 5-foot-9 freshman quarterback who grew to be 6-foot-2 by his junior year. He was "all knees and elbows," according to coach Clay Iverson, but he was determined and still growing.

As a senior he was a defensive end and tight end, and he earned a scholarship to Central Michigan University on offense in 2007. He played one season there but didn't feel quite right, so he went home to the University of Wisconsin to try out on defense.

Watt made the cut and was named a Second Team All-American in 2010. The Houston Texans drafted him 11th overall in 2011, and in his first season he helped the team go from 30th in the NFL in team defense all the way to second. He also had 3.5 sacks and an interception return for a touchdown in two playoff games.

In 2012 Watt took the league by storm, leading the NFL with 20.5 sacks and winning the Defensive Player of the Year award. In 2014 he did both again!

The second time his Defensive Player of the Year nomination was a clean sweep of the ballots, the first time in history that had happened. He was also second to Aaron Rodgers in league MVP voting, earning 13 of the 50 votes, the most a defensive player had received since 1999.

Dominating America's most popular sport does have its drawbacks. Watt tries to visit young patients at Houston hospitals without anyone knowing, but word gets out quickly and he's swarmed. He also has an assistant buy his groceries for him — not because he's too important to run errands, but because his good nature would have him talking with every fan along the way. And even though his neighbors love him, they asked him to stop handing out candy at Halloween because of trick-or-treater chaos.

The upside of fame is the chance to play himself on the TV show *The League* and hang out with Hollywood stars. "If I look at it through the eyes of a kid from Pewaukee," says Watt, "I'm thinking, 'There's no way this is happening.'"

But that scrawny kid grew up to be the 6-foot-5, 289-pound man who leads all players in sacks, quarterback hits and tackles for a loss since entering the NFL.

He is, in the words of former Texans coach Wade Phillips, "the perfect football player."

THAT'S OFFENSIVE!

In 2014, Watt had five touchdowns — three receiving, one on a fumble recovery and one from an interception. He was the first defensive lineman since 1944 to have five touchdowns in a season.

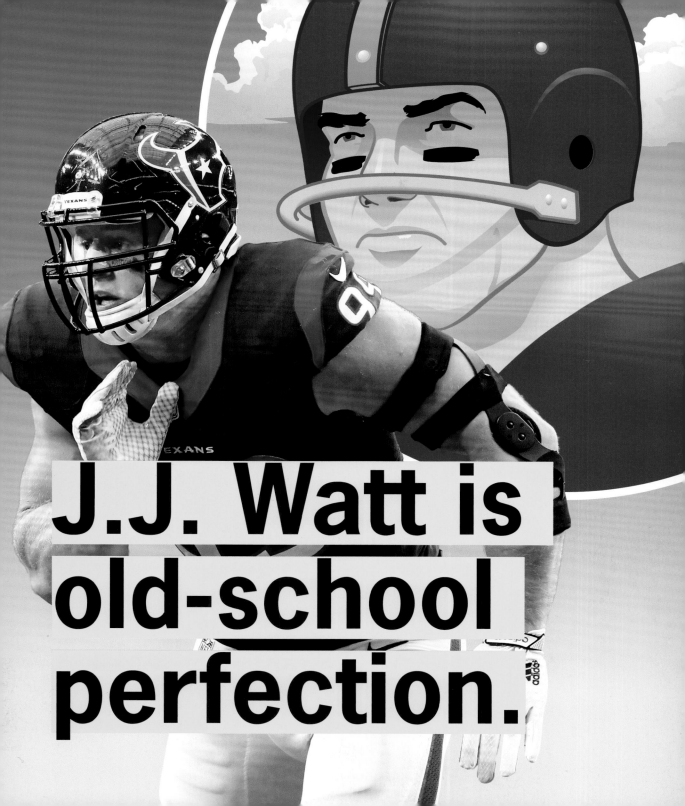

J.J. Watt is old-school perfection.

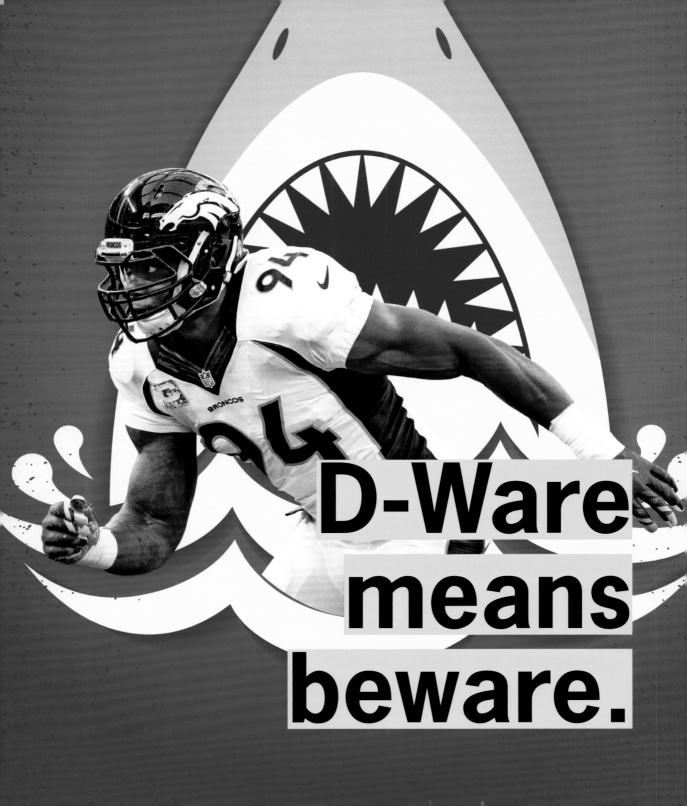

D-Ware means beware.

DeMarcus Ware
Denver Broncos
Linebacker

DeMarcus Ware spent a lot of his childhood at the Boys & Girls Club in Auburn, Alabama, when he had nowhere else to go. It's where he met Heisman Trophy winner and future NFL and MLB star Bo Jackson, as well as members of the Auburn University football team. They came in to spend time with the kids, and it's something that he never forgot.

When he was a student at Auburn High School, Ware sold soft drinks at Auburn University games. A star on offense and defense on his high school team, he dreamt of being down on the field wearing a Tigers' uniform like his heroes. But Ware ended up at the only college that recruited him — Troy University — and when he entered the NFL draft in 2005 he was seen as a "tweener": stuck between a defensive end and an outside linebacker. Projected to go in the second round, the Dallas Cowboys had a little more faith and took him with the 11th overall pick.

It paid off. Ware led the NFL in sacks in 2008 with 20.0 and again in 2010 with 15.5. He was just the fifth player to top the league more than once.

Ware made the Pro Bowl and the All-Pro team seven times in his nine years in Dallas and is the franchise leader in sacks, but the Cowboys released him after an injury-filled 2013 season.

The Denver Broncos believed in Ware's powers of recovery though, and in his first season in Denver, at the age of 32, he had 10.0 sacks and made it back to the Pro Bowl for the eighth time. His eight appearances are the most by any defensive player in the NFL today.

"All he needed to do is get healthy," says Denver teammate C.J. Anderson. "You are talking about a [future] Hall of Famer, one of the best of all time."

Ware also embraced his new community in Colorado, and he was one of the finalists for the NFL's first Sportsmanship Award in 2015. He helps out at the Boys & Girls Club of Metro Denver, taking the kids shopping for holiday gifts and to movies or just being around to play games and offer advice.

"I tell [the kids], I came from where you came from. I was in your shoes," says Ware. "[The kids] look up to you knowing that you had the same circumstances, came from where they come from, and they actually can have a better connection with you because they feel like 'If he can do it, I can do it.'"

It's unlikely any of them will grow up to be a 6-foot-4, 258-pound NFL superstar, but they will remember the one who cared enough to get to know them.

SACK MACHINE | Ware is second in NFL history with 0.81 sacks per game in his career. Only Hall of Fame defensive end Reggie White has more (0.85/game).

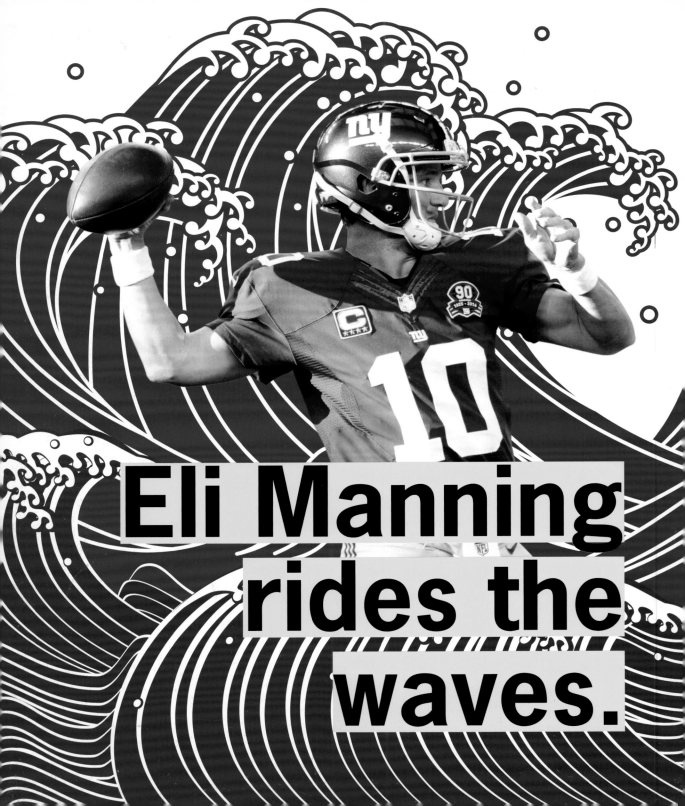

Eli Manning rides the waves.

Eli Manning
New York Giants
Quarterback

Eli Manning is the franchise quarterback for one of the most historic teams in the biggest sports market in the entire United States. Not many could handle the bright spotlight and pressure, but he's been there for over a decade and won Super Bowls and postseason MVP awards. And despite his greatness, Manning still can't get respect.

If he wasn't so cool, that kind of thing might bother him. He was nicknamed "Easy" when he was growing up in New Orleans, a.k.a. the Big Easy.

Pro quarterbacks run in the family. His dad, Archie, was the Saints' quarterback in the 1970s, and Eli's older brother, Peyton, owns numerous quarterback records. Peyton has been named the NFL's regular season MVP a staggering *five* times. In many ways, Eli plays in Peyton's shadow.

But Eli has always managed to take everything in stride. "As laid back and easygoing as you'll see around," says Frank Gendusa, who coached the Manning boys at Isidore Newman School in New Orleans.

Eli followed in Peyton's footsteps as quarterback there and as a first overall pick in the NFL, but in 2011 — with Peyton out with injury for the entire season — Eli stepped out of the shadows and threw for the sixth-most yards in NFL history. Even that wasn't enough, though, as both Tom Brady and Drew Brees threw for more yards, and each broke the single-season passing record.

Brees out-dueled Manning again in 2015 in a 52–49 loss to the New Orleans Saints. Manning threw for six touchdowns; Brees threw for seven. Falling just short has created the impression that Eli isn't among the best NFL quarterbacks.

The notion that Eli can't outperform the biggest stars also meant that no one gave the Giants much of a chance in Super Bowl XLII against Brady and the Patriots in 2007. But Manning wasn't intimidated. On their final drive of the championship, he took the Giants 83 yards for a touchdown and a 17–14 victory. Manning was named Super Bowl MVP.

The Giants and Manning made it to their second Super Bowl in five years when they were back in the title game following the 2011 season. It was a rematch with the Patriots, and Manning got the better of Brady again and earned his second MVP award.

Now that Peyton has retired a champion, Eli is the only Manning left in the league. Given that he's twice taken down Brady and has one more Super Bowl win than Brees, hopefully the New York Giants quarterback will start getting the respect he deserves.

A GIANT AMONG MEN

Manning was named the Giants' Walter Payton Man of the Year four times — in 2007, 2008, 2011 and 2012 — for excellence on the field and in the community. He was also recognized as one of New York's "Top 20 Philanthropists Under 40" in 2015.

Jason Witten
Dallas Cowboys
Tight End

Jason Witten has missed one game in more than 200 contests in his NFL career, and that was in his rookie season when he broke his jaw. Since then, he's played through 28 or so injuries, including a tear in his spleen in 2012 that could've killed him. His toughness is in his DNA, passed down by his grandfather Dave Rider.

In the 1950s, Rider played a high school season on two broken ankles, and at the University of West Virginia he took off a full-leg cast to play. After that he worked in coal mines and coached high school football for 40 years. Rider also helped raise the three Witten boys, teaching them to keep going, no matter what. He also taught them respect and kindness.

Jason was the youngest and the best player in the family. He was a consensus All-American in high school at linebacker, and he started as a lineman at the University of Tennessee. His switch to tight end came about when the Volunteers needed him to fill a roster spot. From there, Witten set single-season school tight-end records in receptions and receiving yards. The Dallas Cowboys selected him 69th overall in the 2003 draft.

By 2004, Witten was dominating the league, leading all NFC tight ends with 87 catches. In 2007 Howie Long named him the "toughest man in the NFL." The honor was in part because of his legendary run against Philadelphia after getting his helmet knocked off by a tackler.

Witten continued his tough act in 2015, when he suffered serious sprains of both ankles and his left knee. As his ankles swelled up and took on shades of purple, it looked like his consecutive-games-played streak was over. But with help from the trainers and his unbreakable spirit (and bones), he was back on the field the following Sunday.

That year he went on to break the Cowboys' record for consecutive games played with his 197th, and he became the second tight end in NFL history with 1,000 career receptions.

"If it's physically possible — and sometimes maybe when it isn't," says fellow Cowboys tight end Jason Hanna, "he's going to find a way, and he's going to play well."

But there's a softer side to the tough tight end. There are Jason Witten Learning Centres in Dallas and Elizabethton, Tennessee, and his Jason Witten Football Camp is one of the country's largest free football programs. After growing up with an abusive father, Witten also started the SCORE Foundation to provide support and assistance for women and children escaping abuse.

"The purpose was to provide a resource for these kids," explains Witten. "To be a male mentor. To be Dave Rider. To be there to inspire, to push, to hug, to listen."

THIS COWBOY CORRALS PIGSKIN
Witten holds the Cowboys' all-time record for receptions, and he has the second-most receiving yards among tight ends in NFL history (behind Tony Gonzalez).

Jason Witten is tough as nails.

Richard Sherman will take you to school.

Richard Sherman
Seattle Seahawks Cornerback

"**U** mad bro?"

That was the Tweet in 2012 that earned Richard Sherman thousands of followers and nearly as many enemies. It came after a game that saw the underdog Seattle Seahawks defeat the New England Patriots. At the time, Sherman's Seahawks were coming off a 7–9 season, and Sherman was a second-year unknown. The Patriots, on the other hand, were defending AFC champions and led by superstar quarterback Tom Brady.

After Seattle beat the Patriots, a picture of Sherman jawing with Brady was put on Twitter with the infamous caption added to it; Sherman later re-Tweeted it.

Growing up in Compton, where the tradition and history of rap music helped shape his verbal game, Sherman steered clear of the Los Angeles neighborhood's notorious gang life by focusing on school and sports. His grades and athletic skill allowed him to attend Stanford University, a school known for demanding good grades. His idol was Muhammad Ali, and, like him, he wanted to have the same combination of athletic talent, sharp mind and social conscience.

Sherman graduated from Stanford with a degree in communications, and he was drafted in the fifth round by Seattle in 2011. He's been a first-team All-Pro every season except his first.

It hasn't all been smooth sailing, however. In the 2013 NFC title game against the San Francisco 49ers, Sherman broke up a pass intended for Michael Crabtree that sealed the game and sent the Seahawks to the Super Bowl. After the play Sherman extended a hand to Crabtree, who pushed him away.

Moments later, Sherman erupted on live TV: "Don't you ever talk about me.… Don't you open your mouth about the best, or I'll shut it for you real quick."

In the aftermath, Sherman was carelessly and unfairly labeled a "thug." He stopped short of apologizing to Crabtree, but he was sorry for overshadowing his team's victory and for putting reporter Erin Andrews in an awkward position.

The Seahawks went on to win Super Bowl XLVIII in dominant fashion, beating the Denver Broncos 43–8.

They returned to the championship the next year, this time facing Brady and the Patriots. Before the game Sherman wrote that he planned to be a better role model for his newborn son. The Seahawks lost Super Bowl XLIX, but showing his maturity, Sherman reached out his hand to congratulate Brady.

Brady was kneeling and taking in the Patriots victory, but he stood up and shook Sherman's hand. It was the sport at its best, with two of the biggest stars showing mutual respect and sportsmanship.

25

TEAM SHERMAN

Sherman has students sign a contract with his foundation, Blanket Coverage. If they agree to improve their grades, keep up their attendance and are good citizens, he'll help them with clothes and school supplies.

Joe Thomas
Cleveland Browns Offensive Tackle

73

No matter what job Joe Thomas ended up doing, he was going to show up every day, work hard and go home to his family. And that's what he does — he just happens to do it in America's most popular sport.

Eligible for the 2007 NFL draft, Thomas was out fishing with his dad instead of sitting with other hopefuls waiting for his name to be called. He had just come off his senior year at the University of Wisconsin, where he had won the Outland Trophy as the nation's top lineman. He knew he was going to be drafted, and he knew he'd give his all to whatever team picked him. He always had. So why fuss?

At Central High School in Brookfield, Wisconsin, Thomas played his heart out, getting time at right tackle, defensive end, tight end, fullback, placekicker and punter. Major colleges heavily recruited him, but he decided to stay close to his family and play at Wisconsin.

Thomas considered declaring for the draft in his junior year, but tearing a knee ligament in the Capital One Bowl temporarily sidelined his NFL dream. After a lot of hard work and rehab, he was named a consensus All-American to go along with his Outland Trophy as a senior, and the dream was alive.

Since then, Thomas' knee — and the rest of his 6-foot-6, 312-pound body — has held up against the grind of the NFL, and he has yet to miss a game in his eight-year career.

There's a simple explanation for his consistency, according to his wife, Annie, whom he met at Wisconsin and asked out on a canoe trip for their first date: "He loves football. He loves his teammates. All the personal success, he's grateful for it. But he's the type of guy who doesn't let the bad or good get to him. I think that's why he's so steady."

Thomas is the anchor of the Browns' offensive line and a leader to the younger players on the team, teaching them football and life skills.

According to former Cleveland quarterback Brian Hoyer, Thomas is a mentor and the face of the franchise in a blue-collar city. "Joe is 'Mr. Brown.'... you see his work ethic, day-in and day-out. When guys have a person like that to look up to, it's a great example."

In 2014 Thomas made the Pro Bowl for the eighth straight year, was named a first-team All-Pro for the fifth time and was voted the Browns' Player of the Year.

"That's pretty humbling," said Thomas of his selection as team MVP. "It never goes to a lineman. It's always the quarterback or a running back or a receiver or somebody on defense "who gets a lot of stats."

It was a mark of respect for his consistency, his toughness and his humility. And when he steps on the field, he's no average Joe.

PRO BALLER | Thomas has been in the Pro Bowl in each of his eight seasons. He's the only offensive lineman in NFL history to be named eight straight years to start his career.

Joe Thomas is the man for the job.

Russell Wilson's persistence pays off.

Russell Wilson
Seattle Seahawks Quarterback

Russell Wilson's dad, Harrison, used to wake him up at 5:30 every morning to work out and run drills, always stressing the importance of poise and preparation. It paid off in his senior year at private Collegiate High School in Richmond, Virginia. Wilson led his football team to the state title, and he batted .467 as the starting shortstop on the baseball team.

Major League Baseball's Colorado Rockies thought he had a future and drafted him in 2010. Wilson had dreams of being like Bo Jackson and Deion Sanders, who both played pro baseball and football. His college football coach at North Carolina State didn't like that idea, so Wilson transferred to the University of Wisconsin. He worked his schedule to play minor-league baseball when the football team wasn't playing, but ultimately he chose the gridiron over the diamond.

A pro football career wasn't a given, however. Even though he set an NCAA record by throwing 379 passes in a row without an interception, Wilson's 5-foot-11 height scared many NFL teams, who thought he was too short. The Seahawks liked what they saw though, and they drafted him in the third round in 2012.

Wilson started all 16 games of his first year and tied Peyton Manning's rookie record with 26 touchdown passes. He set a franchise record with a 100.0 quarterback rating — the second highest by a first-year player in NFL history.

In 2013 the Seahawks won 11 of their first 12 games and beat Manning and the Denver Broncos 43–8 to win Super Bowl XLVIII. Wilson completed 72 percent of his passes, with two touchdowns and a 123.1 passer rating.

He hung out with Barack Obama and Justin Bieber, Beyoncé and Ben Haggerty, a.k.a. Seattle rapper Macklemore. He'd gone from too small to a megastar in 24 months. The Texas Rangers also picked up his baseball rights, and he's twice participated in their spring training.

In 2014 the Seahawks made their way back to the Super Bowl, and with only a few yards between him and back-to-back titles, Wilson had his go-ahead touchdown pass intercepted and the New England Patriots won Super Bowl XLIX 28–24. Speaking like a true professional, Wilson took "full responsibility" for the play.

That kind of maturity is why Seahawks coach Pete Carroll drafted Wilson and trusts him to lead the team. "He is just as complete a person as you could hope to be working with," says Carroll.

Wilson gives the credit to his dad and his mom, Tammy: "They talked to me about my education and how important that was in terms of my work ethic, in terms of my discipline, in terms of respecting people. Those are the lessons that I learned a lot, from a young age."

JUST WIN, BABY!

From 2012 to 2014, Wilson won 36 regular-season games, the most by a starting quarterback in his first three seasons in the Super Bowl era (that is, since 1966). He won 42 including the playoffs, the most combined wins ever in a quarterback's first three seasons.

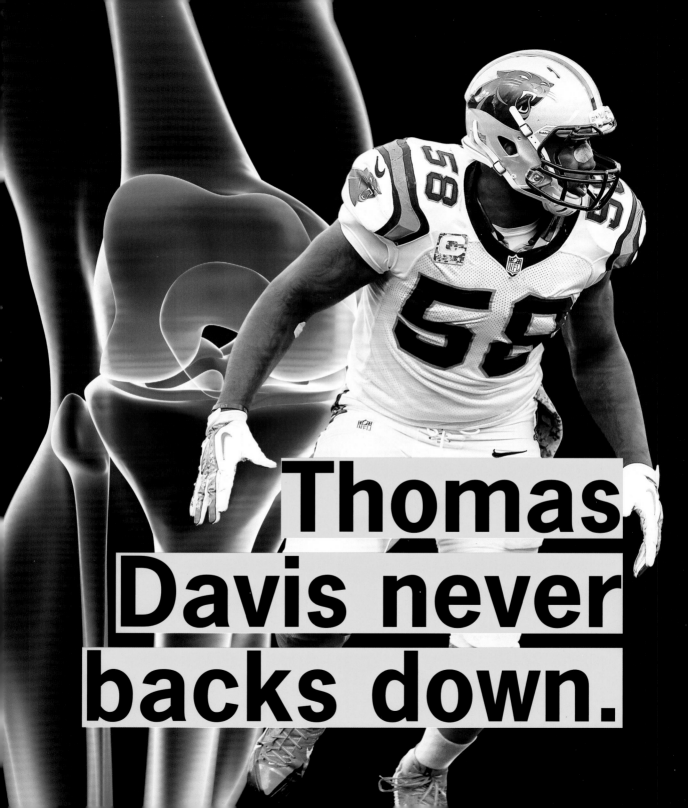

Thomas Davis never backs down.

Thomas Davis
Carolina Panthers
Linebacker

For many players, a torn knee ligament, like an anterior cruciate ligament (ACL), can seriously hurt their career, maybe even end it. Between 2009 and 2011, Thomas Davis tore the ACL in his right knee three times!

The third time he was ready to retire. No NFL player had ever come back from three ACL tears on the same knee. In fact, no professional athlete of any kind had done that.

For Davis to have a chance to keep playing, doctors took parts of his hamstring tendon and patellar tendon on both knees to repair the right knee. He didn't have much left to give, but he wasn't willing to give up.

Davis learned to be mentally strong as a kid in Shellman, Georgia. He remembers wishing that he had someone to help him face his problems.

He participated in sports to help him cope with an unstable home life, and he played eight positions on his high school football team. That kept him away from the gangs and drugs that some of his friends were getting into.

College teams thought he was too small to make it to the next level, but he made the most of his only scholarship offer, becoming an All-American at the University of Georgia on the way to being drafted in the first round by the Carolina Panthers in 2005.

Since returning from his third knee surgery in 2012, he's had three consecutive seasons of more than 100 tackles. He's now second on the Panthers' all-time tackles list, and in 2013 he had a career-high 151 tackles, to go with four sacks and two interceptions. Davis was also one of three finalists for the Walter Payton

58

Man of the Year Award, which recognizes a player's community service and playing excellence.

In 2014 he helped the Panther's defense set an NFL playoff record for fewest yards allowed, giving up only 78 against the Arizona Cardinals, and this time he won the Walter Payton Award. Davis was recognized for his work with his Defending Dreams Foundation, which he started in 2007 to help underprivileged kids. The foundation gives out more than $500,000 in financial aid annually. There are also leadership camps, holiday meals, gifts — and football, of course.

"Kids can learn a lot about life through athletics," says Davis. "It's one of the things I had growing up that really helped me make it through."

The Panthers had their best season ever in 2015, and Davis got the recognition he deserved for being a centerpiece of one of the best defenses in the league. But Davis is more concerned with helping the next generation reach their full potential.

Derek, one of the many kids he's mentored, said it best: "I ran into some trouble. He taught me it [wasn't the] end. You get bumps. You get over them."

BACK TO SCHOOL

Davis left school early to go to the NFL, but he returned six years later to earn his degree and keep a promise to his grandmother.

Tyron Smith
Dallas Cowboys Tackle

77

Legendary basketball coach John Wooden said, "The true test of a man's character is what he does when no one is watching."

It means that when the only person making sure you do the right thing is you, do you still work hard and make the right choices?

In Tyron Smith's case, he's a huge man who does his best work out of the spotlight. He plays for the Dallas Cowboys, America's most popular team, but, as a tackle on the offensive line, Smith's hard work can go largely unnoticed. It's other people who get the benefit — and with Smith, it's been this way since he was a little kid.

From an early age he and his siblings worked in his family's cleaning business. They'd drive hours from their home in Los Angeles to prepare new houses for their first owners. After working through the night the family would get home at four or five in the morning, and young Tyron would then leave for school at eight.

In elementary school, Smith was too busy cleaning to play football, but by the time he got to Rancho Verde High in Moreno Valley, it was hard to ignore his size and skill. It earned him a scholarship to the University of Southern California, where he was an All-American and the conference's top offensive lineman.

Smith was drafted ninth overall in 2011 by the Dallas Cowboys — the first time in 30 years the team had picked an offensive lineman in the first round.

At 20 years old, Smith was the youngest player in the NFL in 2011. He started all 16 games of his first season at right tackle and allowed only three sacks.

Offensive linemen are the biggest men on the field and do the hardest work with the least amount of fame. The Cowboys know what they have in Smith though, so they signed him to a 10-year contract in 2012.

He moved to the left tackle position in 2012, a promotion to protect quarterback Tony Romo's blind side, and in 2014 Romo owed Smith and the offensive line a huge thanks for his career highs in touchdowns and quarterback rating. Running back DeMarco Murray was also grateful as he led the NFL in rushing. The payoff for Smith was his first trip to the playoffs and spots on the Pro Bowl and All-Pro teams.

Smith is a quiet leader who displays wisdom beyond his years. It's why players just a year or two younger look up to him, including defensive end Randy Gregory, whom Smith is happy to mentor.

"I just know how important it is to get help from older guys," Smith says, "so any kind of questions or extra work [Gregory] needs I'm always there [to help]."

Smith's talent has earned him millions; his character earns him respect.

THE DOG DAYS OF DALLAS

Smith and his girlfriend have five rescue dogs, and they created a fundraising calendar with Cowboys players hanging out with dogs to benefit a local shelter.

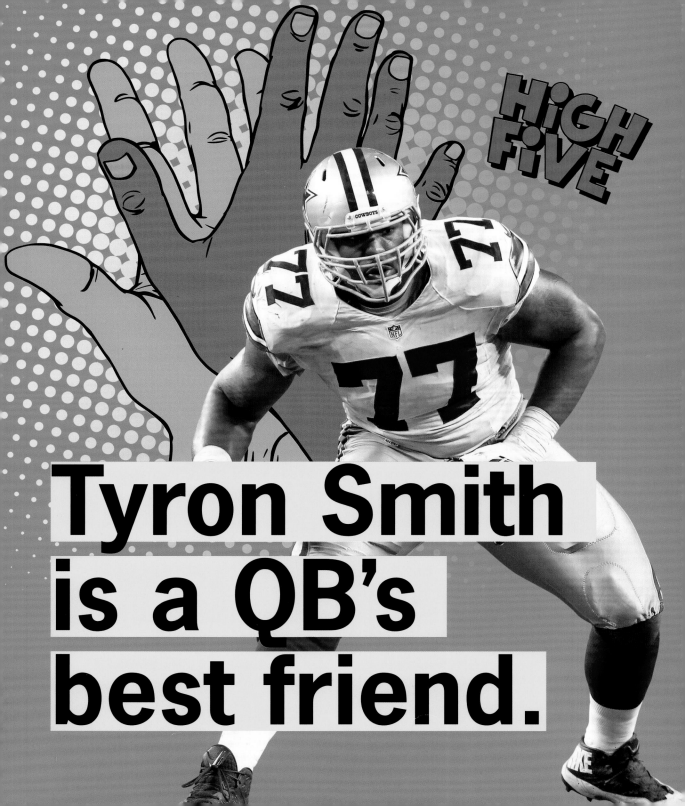

HIGH FIVE

Tyron Smith is a QB's best friend.

Photo Credits

Icon Sportswire
Hector Acevedo 17 (Brady), 58; James Allison 54; Justin Berl 3; Zach Bolinger 24, 48;
Jim Dedmon 29; Andrew Dieb 5, 53, 63; Allen Fredrickson 16 (Favre); Rich Gabrielson 17
(Manning); Daniel Gluskoter 5, 20, 32, 38 40, 44, 60; Rich Graessle 37; Rich Kane 57;
MSA 23, 30, 64; Albert Pena 50; William Purnell 43; Cliff Welch 34, 47; Zumapress 5, 27

Library of Congress Archives
LC-DIG-hec-29339: 13

Associated Press
AP Photo 14; NFL Photos 7, 15; Paul Spinelli 16 (Marino); Greg Trott 6

Shutterstock
Alphabe 50 (background); Anikei 23 (background); Agor2012 37 (background); Aurielaki
9 (field); Bearsky23 10-12 (uprights); Beliavskii Igor 35; Denniro 31, 42; Doodle 9 (referee);
Eatcute 8 (stopwatch); Elgreko 33 (background); Enterlinedesign 39; Halimqd 52;
Happymay 25; Iconic Bestiary 41, 61; Illustratiostock 8 (field, uprights); Jesadaphorn 51;
Julianna Million 53 (background); Kavalenkava Volha 62; Klerik78 8 (first down markers);
Kozoriz; Yuriy 40 (background); Macrovector 26 (hands); Marina Sun 54 (background);
Michael Jaszewski 47 (background); MJgraphics 45; MSSA 58 (background); Natsmith1,
44 (background); NotionPic 21; OnBlast 55; Orin 34 (background); Patrimonio designs ltd
56, 57 (background); Reno Martin 36, 59; RomanYa 27 (background); Sdp Creations 32;
Sebastian Kaulitzki 60 (background); Sentavio 9 (players on field); Steinar 9, 46 (touchdown), 29 (background); Studiostoks 63 (background); Takiwa 20 (background); Tancha
48 (background); TesL 10-12, 26 (football); Toonstyle.com 24 (heads)

Cover
Daniel Gluskoter/Icon (Charles, Fitzgerald, Rodgers)
Patrimonio designs ltd/Shutterstock (background)
Cliff Welch/Icon (Watt)

Back Cover
Hector Acevedo/Icon (Wilson)
MSSA/Shutterstock (Wilson background)
William Purnell/Icon (Houston)
Zumapress/Icon (Brown)